THE DOUBLE LIFE OF CLOCKS

THE
DOUBLE LIFE
OF CLOCKS

Helen Ivory

BLOODAXE BOOKS

ISBN: 1 85224 594 8

First published 2002 by
Bloodaxe Books Ltd,
Highgreen,
Tarset,
Northumberland NE48 1RP.

www.bloodaxebooks.com
For further information about Bloodaxe titles
please visit our website or write to
the above address for a catalogue.

Bloodaxe Books Ltd acknowledges
the financial assistance of Northern Arts.

Cover printing by J. Thomson Colour Printers Ltd, Glasgow.

Printed in Great Britain by
Cromwell Press Ltd, Trowbridge, Wiltshire.

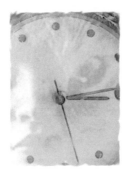

Acknowledgements

Acknowledgements are due to the editors of the following publications in which some of these poems first appeared: *Ambit*, *New Writing 10* (Picador/British Council, 2001), *Reactions* (Pen&inc, 2000), *Reactions 2* (Pen&inc, 2001) and *Spiked*.

I would like to thank the Society of Authors and their judges for an Eric Gregory Award in 1999; George Szirtes for making it all seem possible; and to Mike for everything else.

Contents

Meow

I have always suspected but now
I know for a fact that I am not a human being.
As children, my sister and I were cats.
We would slink around the house,
pause, scratch at fleas and demand our mother
feed us saucers of milk on the kitchen floor.

Now, my sister was only playing.
Her movements were not fluid,
and her meows were unconvincing.
Dolly, the family cat and I would laugh
at her as we washed our faces together.
My Mother was unaware of our rapport.

I was ten years old when my Mother took Dolly
away in a cardboard box. I never saw her again.
Every night, I scratched at the back door
to be let out so I could be with Dolly.
From then on, I only spoke in cat language.
My Mother was at first angry and then upset.

When I was fifteen my Mother took me
away in a cardboard box. I never saw her again.
Every day I am bought food on a plastic plate.
They no longer leave a knife and fork.
At night I call to Dolly in our own language and sometimes
she comes to me. We wash our faces together.

Letter to Her Husband

My Darling,
I have tried to write this letter once before,
but the words come out as blocks.
Grey buildings, tenements in squares that go round and round
repeating, repeating, repeating.

My Darling,
I have tried to write this letter once before.
Will you come and see me soon?
It is Sunday again. It is cold. Too. Again.
When did I last see you?

My Darling,
I have tried to write this letter once before.
Today is Sunday again. The woman with the Devil's eyes
brought cold water to wash with.
She watches until I have finished.

My Darling,
I have tried to write this letter once before,
but in my head it is sunshine
and these words are just shadows.
Will I see you next Sunday?

Correspondence

The postman is keeping my letters.
I know this by the way he looks at me.
That all-knowing smirk.

He knows how much you love me.
I do not know how he knows this
because I didn't know that anyone else

knew our private language.
Unless you taught him. Is that it?
Thinking again, you wouldn't have done that.

We have made promises, you and I.
We're true blue, me and you.
Maybe he's cracked the code.

This worries me.
I'm sending this note via carrier pigeon
as the postman clearly cannot be trusted.

I will come to see you at midnight on Saturday as usual,
but I will be in disguise this time –
he follows me everywhere.

Pacemaker

So I'm running along this road,
really running.
Running properly with all the gear;
the lycra, the air trainers, everything.

It's getting dark,
but I can make out the road
and trees either side of me.
My breathing's going fine

although my lungs kill a bit
'cos the air is so cold.
Anyway, I get the feeling
there is someone right behind me.

I look and it's too dark to see,
but I know there's someone there.
So I pick up the pace a bit.
The adrenaline kicks in about now

and I feel like I can do a marathon.
By the time I get to the end of the road
I've lost him, I don't know where,
there wasn't anywhere he could have gone

except through the trees.
This freaked me out a bit,
so the next day I go in broad daylight.
Not many people use this road,

it's more of a track really,
so my footprints are there from the day before.
When I get to the bit where there was
someone behind me,

there aren't any other prints except mine.
But there seem to be too many of mine.
For the rest of the track there are two sets of prints
with exactly the same imprint as my trainers.

A Curious Thing

This morning, I woke to find that
I had shed a skin.
Stranger still;
I was beside myself.
Literally and metaphorically both.
I looked across the pillow
where my twin lay sleeping.
A translucent barely there shape
formed around the contours of my bones.
She slept soundly and peacefully,
unaware she was without structure.
She seemed to hover at least an inch from the bed
and possessed all the tragic beauty
of a pre-Raphaelite painting;
part angel, part daguerreotype.
And now her breathing
fills every room of the house
with the sound of the sea.
It laps gently around the stairwell,
staining the carpet, peeling the wallpaper.

Looking for Angels

He awoke to the sound of angels
singing softly in his ear.
He looked about him
but there were no angels to be seen.

They could be shy, that's it,
hiding in cupboards
or in the adjoining bathroom,
maybe he should look in there.

When he displayed an active interest
in their whereabouts,
they stopped singing.
And now silence rings through his head

like a telephone, unanswered.

Orangeness of Oranges

A man picked up the telephone
ringing below the surface of the road
where the electricity board
were laying down cables.
It had been ringing for a long time.
Nobody heard it, except that man.
He had heard it the night before
on his way home from work.
The sound came with him to the house.
Its urgency kept him awake all night.
The next morning he could not walk past it again.
He lifted the receiver to his ear
and heard the voice.
It was similar to his own voice, but more earthy.
Far deeper.
It came from a long way away.
The line crackled to indicate this.
What the voice said cannot be written down.
That is to say, it did not speak in words.
Words are easy. They can be written down like so.
No, the voice spoke directly to the man's mind.
It made him see and feel things
he had never seen or felt before.
It even made him appreciate oranges.
(A fruit that had often bored him in the past
because of the preparation involved.)
And now he is able to savour
the orangeness of oranges.
Let the juice fill his senses
with its bitter sweetness.
Let himself be reminded
there is nothing on earth like this.

Dreams

It came to me like a memory.
A strange feeling. I will try to explain.
I dreamt I was alive again.
How can this be

I have slept for a hundred years.
I dreamt (did I dream?)
that I walked to the open window
and saw children playing in the sunshine.

I could actually feel the sun warm my face
and the breeze tickle hairs on my arms.
I dreamt (did I really?)
that I tasted water,

felt its coolness slide right down to my stomach.
And then I dreamt that I woke up,
that I wasn't dreaming.
I cannot be sure of this,

but in my sleep I felt water boiling inside me.
It's hard to explain,
because then, all I could do was watch,
as my body writhed, tying

itself up in sheets.
I could not feel my skin purpling
or smell the thunder that seemed
to be trapped in my skull.

Losing Track

I'd been counting raindrops to tell the time.
At about four a.m. it began to snow so softly
I lost all track of where I was.
Minutes blurred into hours blurred into days
until a whole century was gone.

I tried to focus on something real
but everything around me was unspeakably white.
It seemed I was cast adrift on my bed,
which floated like an iceberg,
glistening in the bright space that was my room.

And I am telling you this
even though you won't believe me.
Even though you tell me that everything's the same,
that time doesn't move like that.
That it's you I should be focusing on.

Hospital Bath

You lower yourself in,
gingerly,
eye catching the emergency cord
you could grab
with a drowning swipe.
And people would come running.
It is their job.

And there's you,
with no bubbles to cover you.
Scrabbling at the sides
like a panicked cat.
Startled claws rip through water,
that sutures together, invisible.

I just wanted to lie flat, you'd say.
Only I forgot to hold my breath
only I forgot to hold my breath.

Why I Don't Use Bubbles

It is enough to consider
the falling and rising of the moon
and the coming and going
of the tide, let alone
the sea changes present within myself.

Take last week for instance.
I was relaxing in a milk and juniper bubble bath
when a vision appeared before me.
It took shape as a bubble that rose
to the surface of the bath and wafted across the room.

Although the warmth of the water surrounded me,
I felt myself to be inside the bubble,
pushing at the coolness of its walls.
I could not change direction
and found myself careering towards the towel rail.

The bubble burst on impact,
and I got out of the bath to see where I had gone.
I scoured the floor, behind the sink,
even lifted the loo seat to see if
I'd fallen down there.

I search for me every day now,
and sometimes, when it is very quiet,
I can feel the crackle of bubbles
nestling inside my skull.

Spin Cycle

I had been suspicious for some time
about the washing-machine.
At first it was the odd sock or handkerchief
that went missing.
Everyday occurrences;
nothing to be concerned about.

But then there was the Aran sweater
put in on gentle spin, never to be seen again.
It was washed on its own
so at the end of the cycle
the drum was entirely empty.
This was a concern.

And this evening I came home to discover
that the curtains had vanished
from the kitchen window.
There was a trail
of soapy suds across the floor
stained with burgundy dye.

I tried to open the washing-machine door
but it was locked tight.
There was a weird echoey gurgle
from deep inside its belly,
causing me to jump,
and back away.

I ran upstairs to find that the duvet
and pillows were also gone
and the floor was awash.
There was a pervasive smell
of *Spring Fresh*
hanging cloyingly in the air.

I could hear an odd clumping sound
on the stairs, getting louder
and the weird echoey gurgle
had become a growl.
It was about then
that you rang the doorbell.

Obviously I couldn't answer the door,
I was cornered upstairs,
so you used your key.
I know it looks strange,
the washing-machine on the landing
and all the carpets soaked.

Yes it must look strange.
No I don't want a cup of tea.

Water

I am bath water.
If you moved a muscle,
I could fill the space you left,
while gently acquiescing
to your new changed shape.

And you would see
your reflection in me
as I traced your contours
like the map of the world.
So I would be your world.

And I would steal so softly
under the surface of your skin,
sculpting waxy waves.
Each time you would grow
just a tiny bit heavier.

You will try to pull the plug
but it would be too late;
for you'd carry
the whole ocean of me,
slowly ebbing at your shores.

Drowning

The day seems too heavy.
The sky is pulled down to meet the land
like a blind on a dirty window.
It brings with it, not clarity nor any particular colour,
or anything you would expect.

The muddy squelch underfoot
is much of the same thing.
If you wanted to run, it would stop you.
Like quicksand, but slower than that;
it would want you to be aware of everything.

Time moves at a different pace,
if indeed it moves at all.
You will not panic when earth covers
your face and stops you breathing.
There will be no feeling to speak of.

Under Water

It has been raining so much that rain has taken me over.
It takes an hour for the house to fill up with water;
at hourly intervals I open the windows to let it out.
Immersion has ruined the carpets,
and I hate to think what it has done to the upholstery.
Ornamental ducks take on a new lease of life.

At first, an indoor swimming pool seemed quite appealing.
Swimming is so good for you,
and to do so much exercise without leaving the house was a boon.
But six days of rain (nobody expected this much rain)
and six days of swimming is extremely tiring.
My skin's gone crinkly too.

The frogs that used to live on the patio
have moved into the back bedroom. It seems to suit them.
I no longer lock the doors, so they come and go as they please.
A family of ducks has been surveying the dining room,
they like the house rules.
If the rain keeps up, I will have to think about charging rent.
I could be sitting on a goldmine.

Outside In

The rain has rained for as long as I can remember.
The gutters are blocked with rotting leaves
and a small lake is forming around the house.
I scan the window, for a lovely fat dove
with a twig in its beak, but see only
crocs and gators tussling for space on the lawn.

These are the days you forget
when the sun is high in the sky.
When the earth is baked so hard
you can't push a fork through it,
and parched leaves fall to the ground,
brittle, ghostlike.

The day's eye closes, and liquefies
into night in big watercolour shapes.
I long to put life into the landscape,
bring it in from the rain, from the dark,
sit it down by the fire and toast marshmallows,
while we wrap ourselves like mummies in warm bath towels,
and I tell it stories about days that begin
at four a.m. with cows mooing at the sun.
But no, it would never believe them,
never in a million years.

The Untreeness of Trees

The trees have forgotten how to be trees.
They have forgotten their voluptuousness,
their collusion with the summer breeze.
They stand in formation along the horizon,
spiky silhouettes on the pale winter sky,
baleful in their nudity, all ribs and angles.

They have taken to scratching on windows
and frightening the children,
to creaking and groaning and upsetting the dogs.
In cities, dark clusters drink cider by the can,
crushing their empties in unswept parks,
muttering archaic words to no one in particular.
They linger on unlit corners,
harassing old ladies, wolf-whistling at girls.

Storm

Last night, the house shock so much
I thought it would be carried away.
Witches on bicycles flew past the window,
engaged in some private joke
making them laugh like drains.

The branch of a tree tapped on the window
for hours and hours and then let itself in.
It made a scene about being ripped untimely
from the trunk by the bully wind.
What did it expect us to do?

On the other hand, the gate rocked on its hinges,
calling to its accomplice
to be freed from mundane duties
as it crashed and crashed against the gate post.

The wind whistled about us
as we tried to watch television:
the pale flat image unaffected.

Hunger

For days and days
a storm had been raging
about the land:
Lifting roofs from buildings,
and throwing them angrily down,
as if it were looking for something.

When it came to our village,
an old man from the next farm
stood in the middle of a field
in the middle of the night
brandishing a scythe.
At the top of his voice, he shouted;
'What is it that you want?'

For a while, the wind was still.
Just a whisper in the treetops,
and then, more fierce than before,
it plunged back down to the ground,
lifted the man by the ankle,
and carried him clean away.

In the hushed night sky,
the moon hung heavily
over the old man's field.
The sharpened arc of the scythe
glinting in the cool, clear light.

The Wind of Forgetting

It came from the desert, they think;
the red wind thick with sand
and the perfumes of a foreign land.
The mountain people saw it first;
a heavy tide, so dense it blocked out the sun.

They threw themselves to the ground
hunkering down against its roar,
covering their eyes and ears.
But the sand buried them entirely
and stole their voices.

In the valley they didn't hear it coming.
This time it swept gently by;
filling the air with a pink haze
that when inhaled
erased every memory.

It came upon the sea people
as a vast cacophony of screams;
the lost and forgotten
all wanting to be heard,
all wanting to be found.

So they left their broken boats
scattered by the wind,
and the sea, running red;
the exact colour and taste of blood,
with the screams still loud in their ears.

And for one thousand years
they wandered the land,
in a red wind thick with sand,
searching for the homes
they knew they once had

in mountains and valleys and seas.

The Ship of Belonging

For years and years he had wandered
the land in search of a name.
It was always on the tip of his tongue
and some nights it woke him
like the sound of an animal
crying out in the darkness.

And then he heard talk of a galleon
that was sunk in a stretch of water
across the other side of the world.
That ship was said to hold riches
more precious than the glitter of jewels
or the promise of gold.

Pirates had first captured and then sunk
it in rage when they found
nothing on board that they wanted.
So it rested on the floor of the ocean;
collecting pearls and sheltering
baby fishes in its hull.

It took him four years to cross the world,
and his nights grew more restless
with the cries of animals.
He found he could no longer speak;
as half-formed words, the shape
of his name, filled his mouth.

He knew exactly where the ship
had foundered by the colour of the water;
by night it glowed a dazzling blue,
and by day shone more brightly than the sun.
Nobody else seemed to notice this,
nor did they feel the music in the air.

It was calling to him; every syllable of sound
sang the name that he'd never heard.
And that moment he knew he must answer;
diving in, he sank deeper, and deeper
into the clear ocean, and bathed
in the light that was warmer than sunshine.

And for the first and last time,
he spoke his name to the oysters
and the fishes that were listening.

Sleeping with the Fishes

When I was a goldfish you never noticed me.
Every day I would watch you eat breakfast.
I knew your favourite cereal, how many times
you would chew before you swallowed each spoonful.

On Tuesdays and Thursdays you worked late.
You bought Chinese food and ate in front of the TV.
This invariably gave you indigestion.
I did worry about you – you always looked so tired.

At night I would circle round while you could not sleep.
I would sing you lullabies that you could not hear.
Sweet tunes to drift you away to a place I would never go,
until the light of morning broke through the dirty window.

When one night you didn't come back from work,
I watched the mail pile up for days, alone in your empty house.
The phone rang once, but I couldn't reach it.
Was it you? Did you phone me? Did you?

I dreamt you chose to swim with me.
You liked the patterns light makes on the surface.
How the world distorts with each turning tide
as icy water soothed your tired eyes.

Clocks on the Rocks

The past is a thing of the past
said the man clocking his stopped watch.
There is only now and it is six o'clock.
He had checked his watch so many times in the past,
more times than he cared to remember.
Time was when time was important,
when he had to be somewhere, somewhen ago.

He decided that six o'clock would be p.m.,
because six in the morning was always too early for him.
Six in the evening, home from work,
gin and tonic, ice and lemon. Perfect.
The ice cracks as it melts, while outside
the gin pink sun rocks steadily around its own clock.

A Few Spiders Short of a Web

First light. Already six spiders
are marching through my room.
Yesterday there were four,
and the day before that there were two.
Mathematics tells us that by next week
there will be fourteen spiders in total.

But if there are not fourteen spiders by next week
we will assume that next week has not yet arrived.
(I do understand the problems associated
with the theory – what does 'next week' mean
if time is measured in the number of spiders present?
I am working on the terminology as we speak.)

Just a few spiders ago, time was measured
in seconds, minutes, hours and so on,
but these are invisible and therefore meaningless.
Spiders, on the other hand, are not invisible;
they are a more tangible solution for
the arachnid-honoured problem of finding
a way to describe the sequential order of things.

How the Mouse Moused the Elephant

I have devised a wonderful account
of how the mouse moused the elephant.
While thinking for some time about this
(as I have done many times before)
I came up with the perfect solution.
To describe my theory, I have used drawings
that work like cartoons in comics.
This shows the precise actions of the aforementioned.

Since the mouse is somewhat diminutive
in comparison with the elephant,
I have suggested in the drawing that he had an axe.
The axe is mouse-sized, so quite small;
it would have little impact on such a beast.
Another problem. But the beauty of my plan
(as the next picture shows) is that when the mouse
actually mouses the elephant, he gets bigger.

The only way to mouse an elephant
is manifestly to stay in proportion with it.
In the drawing of the actual mousing,
I wanted to use red paint to show it graphically.
HB pencil is not dramatic enough for such a scene.
Alas, I feel that some of the violence has been omitted,
but I was not allowed any more materials.
Given the right tools I'm sure

I could more graphically illustrate my point.

Gift Horse

Can you imagine my utter frustration
when I found that next door had removed
all of the flowers I had planted for them?
Anybody else would have been overjoyed
to be greeted by a host of golden daffodils
at such an otherwise undecorative time of year.

I did it when they were on last on holiday.
They didn't ask me to look after the cat this time,
so I took it upon myself to do them another favour.
I thought it only as a mark of respect that
I planted them on the grave of poor Tiddles,
or whatever its name was.

And what is wrong with flowers, may I ask?
I can understand that they send the fruitcake back
uneaten, because that's not always everybody's
cup of tea. A bit too heavy, granted,
but my fruit never sinks. I take great pride in that fact.
However, there is no pleasing some people.

It's not as if the cat ever spent much time with them.
Always digging up somebody else's garden.
It wasn't a mouser either. One of those long-haired ones,
didn't see the point of it really. Never mind,
I shall have to think of something else to give them.
I'll take it round later when they're all asleep.

Lost Weekend

She lost a whole weekend in that house.
Time became forever and no time at all,
at about eight o'clock on Friday.
The sun shone through the night
and the birds sang so loudly
it was impossible to sleep.

On Saturday (we will call it Saturday)
the ghost that had stolen her watch
last week – and her purse the week before –
was parading around the upstairs bedrooms
wearing the perfume she could not find.

Sunday arrived suddenly and unexpectedly
after Saturday with no night in between.
Having spent an indeterminate amount of time
cleansing the upstairs bedrooms
of what used to be her favourite perfume,
she lay down on her unmade bed
while the house with its slow breathing
closed around her, filling her lungs.

A Little Night Music

The first odd thing I noticed
was when I got into the bath
and the water-level didn't rise.
Doors became a problem too.
I couldn't seem to turn the handle
and had to wait for someone to open it
and follow them in like a shadow.

Shopping became a nightmare.
I spent hours in queues waiting to be served
when the people either side of me
were ordering bread or paying for apples.
It was around this time I completely lost my appetite,
which was just as well under the circumstances.

What bothered me most was when dogs started to bark
and when children had fits of tears when I was around.
For this reason I began staying in.
I would sometimes venture out at night,
but only when there was a full moon,
or I'd be falling down all over the place.

The final straw came when people moved into my house.
Can you believe the cheek of it?
They would constantly complain how cold it was,
with the central heating up full blast,
while I was so hot I couldn't bear it
and had to keep opening the windows.

They began throwing my furniture out.
There was a skip outside piled sky high with all my worldlies.
When they went to bed I would carry them back in again.
I seemed to have developed a super-human strength
and could even move the piano on my own.
And it was still in tune when I got it back in the parlour.

After nights and nights of moonlight sonatas
and a little night music for good measure,
I have finally got the place back to myself.
You have to be proactive rather than reactive in this life,
there's no sense in being a doormat for the world and his wife.
I could get used to this kind of power,
I've always fancied living in one of those big houses on the hill.

Phantasmagoria

The other day Mrs Patterson
passed away.
She was not ill,
there was no pain even,
and she did not die.
She just ceased to be.

She did not realise this had
happened until later that same day
when Mr Patterson came home from work
and did not see her.
She cooked supper,
he ate it, but did not see her.

At first, she was a distant memory,
and then he began to doubt that
she ever existed.
He had come to the conclusion
that his entire marriage had been
a phantasmagoric experience.

In this meantime, Mrs Patterson
hung around the house looking
more pallid by the day.
Cobwebs sutured her
to the kitchen sink until it was hard
to tell where she finished and it started.

Mr Patterson decided to sell
the house. It was impossible for
him to understand why a single
man would need such a big house.
With the money he bought a yacht
in which he plans to sail around the world.

Tapestry

She began the tapestry late one night
when her husband was asleep.
Insomnia drove her downstairs,
while the sound of his breathing
filled the room like the sea on a stormy night.

Her colours were muted at first.
Soft, feminine, understated;
a reflection of her wardrobe.
Her stitches were faltering,
feeling her way with the new medium.

As night edged towards morning,
the sound of the sea coursing through the stairwell
prompted a change in her colour scheme.
The stitches too, became bolder, more confident,
as she learnt to ride each crashing wave.

As dawn approached she worked faster,
spurred on by the reddening sky,
her frenzied needle drawing blood.
When sunlight flooded the room,
only then was she able to see her image;
a small boat floundering on a blood-green sea.

Her Big Day

On Monday, she went into town
to buy some fabric for a wedding dress.
A fairytale wedding dress,
with all the ribbons and bows it would hold.

After much deliberation, she chose a length
of dusty white silk and some real Victorian lace.
It was all very expensive, but she'd been saving
for twenty five years for her big day.

At home she set to work cutting the fabric
from a pattern she had dreamed up over the years.
The fabric was easy to cut, she could cut it in her sleep,
as she'd done on many sleepless nights.

She worked solidly through the night,
unaware, for once, of the time
and that her husband hadn't come home.
It was noon on Tuesday when she looked at the clock.

The dress, of course was a perfect fit,
the bride looked stunning as she carried her suitcases
over the threshold and away from the house,
looking back only once to unhitch her trail from the wisteria.

Fairytale

If I was my boyfriend
I would not forget my birthday
or how to use a knife and fork.

If I was my boyfriend
I would not get drunk
and eat all of the cheese.

Or pretend to be asleep
while mice marched through the kitchen,
looking for bits of cheese
that just happen to be lying around.

If I was my boyfriend,
I would definitely treat me like a princess,
unless of course, I needed to feel independent
like a modern girl should.

If I was my boyfriend,
I would eat fire, move mountains, write operas,
swim the channel, change the world,
and serenade me from under my window
while I plaited my hair in a strong
thick rope for me to climb.

The Fire Dress

And when the fire began to
consume the fleshy wood,
she began to add more to feed
its whetted appetite.

The hotter the flames became,
the more wood she added,
spurred on by its passion.
Still she added more.

And then, let God be my witness,
she took the fire into her hands
as if it were the finest silk,
and wove a dress for herself.

A long, flowing dress of
golden orange fire.
A dress more beautiful
than any I have ever seen.

Not content with that,
she took another ball of fire
into her hands,
turning it this way and that.

A magnificent horse reared
from those flames.
It gnashed and writhed,
barely containing its spirit.

And all at once,
she leapt upon that beast and rode away,
leaving a trail of burning grass
that would later turn to black.

Her sleep invaded by unwelcome thoughts

Her sleep invaded by unwelcome thoughts,
she began moving among nocturnal shapes
and came to rest in a pool of moonlight
wiggling her toes in its liquidity,
as it painted shades of blue and Naples yellow on her skin.

Outside, gunfire broke the spell of silence
as men tracked down the season's rabbits.
Lights followed them into the darkness,
the smell of gunshot staining the air.

She saw herself running through fields,
her legs ripped by brambles, tearing through grass.
Where a hundred pairs of glassy eyes stared
blindly at the stars, willing them all to go out.

Night-vision

It's late. Darkness fills the room
with an unquenchable desire for sunshine.
Soon there is nothing but the night.

A stream of moonlight trickles through
the open window across the bedroom floor.
I follow to the stairwell and watch it

bounce from each step. It coaxes me
to the door, caressing my toes with silver kisses.
I open the door and step out into the blue landscape.

Moving further into the night, there is only water.
The moon's image floats, billowing in the breeze.
I dive in and swim below the surface of the moon.

Ice. A string of pearls twists itself around my throat.
Brittle weightlessness takes me beyond gravity
to a place where it's possible to forget who I am.

Nightscene

The Garden is unrecognisable this evening.
I lie in the middle of the lawn, dried leaves in my hair
and the damp river smell takes my senses below ground.

I look up and see nothing but sky. The shades
of milky black and blue move in and out of one another,
reflecting the patterns of my thought.

A frog negotiates the patio, escaping into the darkness
of an August evening. I imagine it crossing my belly.
It feels like gentle rain.

The cows in my garden swim in moonlight

in paths mapped out by the stars.
They move in single file,
slow silhouettes in the moonlit dark.
Their breath warms the air in clouds
and low music fills the air,
tugging at the edges of my dreams.
I breathe in the scent of their skin
and see the stars reflected in their eyes.

We are navigated to pastures
that sing with the sounds of the night.
I stand still as the cows pass me by.
They are silent now, and seem to move as one,
padding softly in the long grass,
dissolving in the space between night and day.
And all day the stars are blinded by the sun.

Chicken by Moonlight

It is November and four thirty in the afternoon.
A late chicken is in the garden;
in about one hour it will be completely dark.

We will assume that she knows this. Even though
she has no wrist-watch (because she has no wrists)
we will hope she reaches her hut before nightfall.

She must be aware of the dangers that darkness
holds for her kind. Its guillotine threatens to fall
anytime now.

The other hens are all in their huts,
securing respectable places on high perches.
They know what's good for them.

And still she struts and scrats by the light of the new moon,
using every last minute of today's free-ranging.
Her shadow is vast. Too big for a chicken.

Infuriation

There is nothing more infuriating than
chasing chickens around in the dark, in the mud.
Especially if it is pouring with rain.
I have just been infuriated
almost beyond redemption.
Sliding and squidging around.
It is no game to them,
they hate it as much as I do.
So why do we do it, each and every night,
with or without the addition of rain?
They want to go inside really.
They don't want to be eaten alive.

Playing Chicken

Late winter, early spring.
The sun casts a wary eye over the chicken-dotted field.
The hens are open to all suggestion of springtime,
urgently dust-bathing in still damp soil.
Orange feathers shine radiantly;
there is no room for ugly, balding chickens on this health farm.
At night they perch in rows, ceiling high,
singing *Keep young and beautiful*
as if chickenfeed were the elixir of everlasting youth.

Picture of a Chicken

The chicken in the picture
has just eaten a cropful of silver beans
she found growing in a neighbour's garden.
The beans (that are not in the picture)
had been cultivated for a special purpose
using age-old propagation methods.

The chickens not in the picture
were scratting around in the farmyard,
waiting for the flying competition.
The prize, offered up by the farmer's wife
a lifetime's supply of corn and kale.
Everyone knows chickens adore that meal.

It is also common knowledge that a hen
can fly no higher than a broomstick.
The chicken in the picture had other ideas.
Previously she had eaten just one silver bean
and found herself able to fly to extraordinary
heights, with a tiny flap of her wings.

From way up in the sky, she was able to spy
the other hens practising flight.
She laughed as one fat hen landed
unceremoniously on her backside
in a flurry of feathers.
The prize, she felt, was already hers.

Hold this image in your mind, if you will,
for it's the last picture we have of her.
Look at me! she cried to the watching crowds,
with her eye on the prize, *Look at me!*
Up and up she soared, till even the hen
with the keenest of sight could see her no more.

Sometimes on a clear night, with a good telescope,
you can pick out her small silhouette on the moon.
And if it's quiet, you can hear her
lamenting her greed for the silver beans,
and despite her repentance,
still longing to return for her prize.

Flight of the Moon Bird

Nobody knew exactly when the moon disappeared,
for the clocks stopped at varying times.
Mostly, the hands stuttered between two and three a.m,
quivering like a mouse's heartbeat.

The tide went out on one side of the world,
yet there was no moon to draw it back;
so it just kept going and going,
till it engulfed the other side of the world entirely.

The sky was a piece of black paper
and the stars winked and glimmered,
fighting to be the brightest night-time light
while people lit torches, to lull the sea back to shore.

By now, time was not a concept; it being just light
or very dark. Fish got bored waiting for the sea
to come back, so those who could, grew wings
and flew away to greener pastures, clearer skies.

Light and very dark went by like this
for some considerable stretch,
till a big gleaming silver bird appeared in the sky
just as it was getting very dark indeed.

That bird held in its beak a luminous balloon
on an airy thread that looked just like the moon.
It billowed slightly now and then,
but the bird held it fast, guiding it through the heavens.

Thus, time began again as watches were wound
and the sea returned to the shore.
New time was not exactly the same as old time
but fishes shed their wings and leapt back in the sea.

And every night that big silver bird carries the new moon
through the sky; a thin skinned balloon
on an airy thread, locked firmly
in its very long and very sharp beak.

The Sky Is Bigger than Usual

I am a tiger prowling the streets at night
feeding on stray dogs and unstreetwise cats.

The sky is bigger than usual tonight
and the clouds hang close to the ground.

It is easy to see the whole universe
from my window to the sky.

Here it is fairly safe;
the moon is a sleepy eye

and the stars don't know I am made of glass,
nor can they see the pictures in my head.

But I know they're out there though, satellites.
Winking from the big dark sky,

sending signals to my brain,
making me tell the most absurd stories.

Narrative

This is my history to date:
I was born in Africa to English parents
and grew up with a lion-cub.
When I was fourteen my parents
were killed in a plane crash.
Very sad. A bad experience.
I was sent to School in England
but I ran away to join the circus.
I now put my head in lions' mouths every day.

My life story, you ask?
I am one of sixteen children
raised on a farm in Ireland.
I went to University in Paris
and learned to paint in watercolours.
In France I am a very famous artist.
I'm surprised you haven't heard of me.
Who did you say you were?

Well Doctor, I'm feeling quite well.
I don't know why you've been sent for.
Did you know I trained in medicine before the war?
Amputations in a tent with no anaesthetic
and gunfire going on all around...
you guys have got it good these days.
No blood on your white coat hey Doc?
But wait there, no, you're my old friend Gerry!
How the hell are you?
What are you doing posing as a mechanic?

In a Former Life I Was an Athlete

In a former life I was an athlete.
That's why I run so much.
That's why I spend hours

on a treadmill, rolling road,
call it what you will.
Going forward, but not really.

Going faster than everybody else
who may as well be stationary,
or dead for all they care.

Inactivity is a strange suicide.
The lazy way out.
Everything slows down, becomes useless.

Especially muscles.
The biggest of these is the heart.
Like unused biceps, the heart shrinks

and becomes weak.
I can tell you this as a fact
because in a former life I was a doctor.

What Am I?

I am God today.
Today I can swim under water,
murky water.

Swim with no need for air.
I can see (because I am God today),
I can see through all the underwater slime.

And because I am God today,
I can create anything –
so I create a man.

Here he is, swimming next to me.
The man will drown because he needs air.
The man drowns.

Because I am God today, I will let this happen.
Tomorrow, if I am still God,
I will make another man.

This time I will make him in my own image.

The Phone Is Ringing

The phone is ringing
but I will not let them in.
Last time they came here
they ate all my food,
then they hid all the plates
and cups and things.

The phone is from a long way away.
If I pick it up it gets closer, and nearer,
till I feel them crawling through my ear.
It is all scratchy until they're in,
and then they make me think that I like
Brussels sprouts, because they are good for me.
But I remember that I don't so I spit them out.
And that makes them cross
and it goes all burny in my head,
so they put ice cream in to make it better.

The phone is still ringing.
And now it is shouting at me
and it doesn't go away when I close my ears.

The Spider Choreographer

Each day there is a new
spider's web in this room.
And each day
I brush it away.

Sometimes it sticks
to my hand.
And at this point,
I am the fly.

It is difficult to free
it from my fingers.
A peculiar dance is needed
to do this.

I swirl my arm around.
Shake my hand loosely
at the wrist.
And then wash my hands.

The spider watches,
eight-eyed.
Tomorrow's dance will
include leg movements too.

Note to the reader: this is not a poem

The pictures are falling from my walls
because the paint is too heavy.
Illusionary landscapes are real landscapes now.

No need for tonality or warmth of colour.
Now I write another poem that nobody will read.
There is loneliness in these words

I tell you the supposed reader in plain terms.
There is no need to hide behind poetry.
I won't try to be clever with you.

Winter

Winter is bigger than I am.
He wears size twelve shoes
and has his suits hand-made in London.

Winter is well dressed.
And I am dressed well. Practically.
Dressed for the cold.

Winter can be stylish for he
does not feel the cold he exudes.
He even wears shades.

Winter has seen more summers,
he understand everything completely.
I don't even know how to keep warm.

It's Like This

What really bothers you,
what keeps you awake
is the way the darkness
follows you home each night;
erasing all the sunshine
like a big black wave
that gets nearer each day.

When November arrives,
you find yourself running home,
the darkness up to your waist
by the time you reach the door.
Your clothes are soaked
as you drag yourself
to the safety of your lamplit room.

And no matter how hard
you try to wring the night-time
from your clothes and from your hair,
you find it seeping in
through cracks in windows
and thick inky puddles of it
around the foot of your door.

And it's like this every year.
And every year you say it will be the last.

The Red Dress

Once again, daylight finds her foetal, but more so.
Sheets knot around her purpling skin
and the ache in her limbs is set fast for the day.

At first, she had tried to wash the pain away,
dissolve it in hot baths,
let bubbles take it far beyond
till their heavy swollen bellies
bring them tumbling to the ground.

These days it is so much a part of her
that amputation would leave phantom suffering.

Sometimes, when she wakes before morning,
the pain drapes loosely around her like a shawl.
It makes her believe she could shrug it off,
just leave it there, like it doesn't belong to her.

Today she wears it like a dress,
so tight, she can barely move.
The red fabric burns her skin
as she reaches for the knife to cut free.

Cleaning Lady

So she tidied the apples
from the orchard floor
until her basket was
filled to the top.

Next she set about
sweeping the dead leaves
into a big pile
and put them into plastic bags.

She scraped the trees
clean of moss
and scrubbed them
till they were lichen free.

There was something
in the shape of the branches,
the way they grew like
spiky fingers.

Something about
the dankness of the orchard,
that way the trees
surrounded her

and took away
her light, her oxygen,
that made her want to
run and keep running.

She pulled the trees out of the ground,
ripping her hands on the bark.
She pulled harder as the roots emerged
from the blackened quiet earth.

Then she gathered them together
in her arms like naughty children
and opened her handbag and put them all in
before carefully closing the catch.

Baggage

After I had finished the coffee
I had so faultlessly ordered by its Italian name,
I looked down at the bag I'd been carrying around all morning.
I did not recognise it. It did not seem to be mine.
Maybe I'd picked it up by accident on the bus, I mused,
while unzipping the zipper.

I delved into the bag and began to examine its contents.
Inside was a driving licence, a cheque book and card,
along with a well thumbed copy of *Madame Bovary*
with pencilled notes on most pages.
All items, to my utter mystification,
seemed to bear my own handwriting.
At this point, I began to doubt my sanity.

Next, I consoled myself that maybe this was
some sort of elaborate practical joke,
with myself as unsuspecting victim.
I looked about me for hidden cameras and the like.
Finding no evidence of such activity,
I had no choice but to throw the bag into the nearest bin,
and use the train ticket I found nestling in my pocket.

I send you this from somewhere hot and sunny,
hope that you are well
and everything is rosy in your garden.
Yours sincerely, etc. etc.

Walking

The urge to keep walking was a physical ache.
Electricity coursed through her limbs,
controlling her every movement as the flies buzzed around
and the sun beat its dizzying spell on her back.

She waded through the long grass
weaving her way through thistles, moving further
and further away from the familiar landscape,
towards the sea which grew bigger with each step.

She didn't notice that she made no footprints
in the sand walking towards the waxing tide,
nor could she feel its briny cold surrounding her,
removing her completely from sight.

The Sea House

She wanted a house by the sea
so with her bare hands
she dug foundations deep,
through rocks, chalk and lime.

She wanted the walls tall
like a lighthouse,
and for her windows to be filled
with nothing but sea.

She wanted a room alive
with music; with the sound
of skylarks and the distant
cries of gulls.

She wanted a bed,
soft as pure white sand;
for the tide to cover her
every night.

And she wanted no more
of the taste of his name
on the tip of her tongue
drowning her every word.

Just Words

We made sentences
out of odd phrases, you and I.
Clumsy structures
that let the rain in.

We built whole
philosophies
on foundations
of air and words alone.

Strange syntaxes
like translated English,
all back to front
and upside down.

And to think
this was our only tongue
when now the words
are chalkdust on my hands.

Particles fall silent
to the ground, as in a dream
or an old photograph
lightly foxed.

The Coat

I made a coat out of words.
I embroidered each letter carefully in black silk.
For the arms, I used mainly verbs;
since arms are "doing" things, this fits perfectly.

For the front panels, I chose oddments,
words that mean nothing except what they say.
As the wearer of the coat would be
unaware of the back panels;

at first they did not seem important,
but upon deeper reflection,
I decided they were the most important of all.
Other people can see your back,

although most of the time the person whose
back it is is completely unaware of it.
With this in mind, I chose words that
speak directly to the outsider.

When the outsider reads the words, he or she
will bear them in mind
when addressing the wearer of the coat.
If this works very well indeed, the outsider

will not even have to address the wearer
of the coat at all, because the words would have said
everything the outsider needs to know, making
further contact with the wearer unnecessary.

Skin of Mirrors

There is a woman walking
through the mountains and valleys.
Her skin is made of mirrors,
and she camouflages herself
in rocks and against the wide open sky;
clouds forming where her eyes would be.

Sometimes, when you are alone;
when you have climbed so high
above the treeline, where there is just rock
and tough-footed deer;
you feel her presence in the cold thin air,
and she is at your shoulder.

To see her would be to see yourself.
To see your eyes, looking down on clouds,
to see your feet, finding footholds
as you go even higher
till there is no sound at all
but the flow of glacial streams.

And now she is so close
your own skin is mirrors;
as you camouflage yourself
in rocks and against the wide open sky;
clouds forming where your eyes once were,
icy streams tricking through your ears.

The Man Who Paints the Sky

It all began when rain fell so hard and long
that every drop of sky fell to the ground.
When there was no more sky,
an empty black space like a vacuum
surrounded the earth,
randomly drawing things in
and throwing them back haphazardly.

People would go to sleep in the desert
and wake to the sound of whalesong
or the bark of an Arctic fox.
Cows rained from the sky in huge herds,
grazing grass to the ground,
leaving rivers of milk
criss-crossing the whole world.

Representatives from every nation
gathered together,
anchoring themselves to the rocks and the trees
that were proving too heavy to move.
They floated around like balloons
and discussed all the ways
to put sky back in the sky.

And so they called upon the world's artists
to paint, from memory, the sky's likeness.
The painter of the most perfect sky
was then unanchored
and immediately sucked into the void;
kicking at the empty space,
paint-brush still in hand.

So now he fills the sky
with great, wide brush strokes
to keep the blackness back.
And if it rains, it's only watercolour
that stains the ground in fat sploshes;
greening up the dullest grass,
muddying the clearest seas.

The Sweetness of Spring

It takes till midday for the sun to rise
over the mountains in October,
and for the three months of winter
it hasn't the strength to rise at all.
Paths become slippery;
gnarled tree roots and wet mossy stones
are hazardous traps for the people
who live thereabouts.
So in winter they tend to stay put.

A chill north wind blew that year,
enquiring at windows and dampening fires.
Nothing could keep it out;
not curtains nor blankets nor furs.
It seemed to creep up on people,
seep under their skin and grip their hearts
till they grew stony cold.
They all fell into a kind of a stupor.
That wind was darker than winter itself.

People just stopped caring;
about their houses, each other and the animals.
They made no more cheese,
collected no more scraps for the sow
who was farrowing late that year.
Birthdays were forgotten
and broken roofs went unrepaired.
All over the valley they stayed in their houses
getting colder and meaner.

And the wind changed, just like that.
The new air smelled of honey
and the sweetness that is spring.
Little by little their hearts unfroze;
they opened their doors,
saw the state of the town
and began mending roofs and the ties of friendship.
Even the sow was helped to rear her young
with such kindness she forgave their neglect.

When the North Wind called upon them again,
they had forgotten the sweetness of spring.
And as the sun set for the last time that year,
they locked their doors and tried to light their fires
as the sly wind chuckled in the grate.

The Brambles in Monet's Garden

There are more brambles in the garden this year,
noted Monet on his pre-breakfast walk.
Work went badly that morning;
his colours and tones were all wrong,
too dark for the time of day.

He could think of nothing but the long thorny shoots
at large in his garden.
He could even hear them growing.
He felt their shadow over him,
pressing him down till he couldn't see.

By late morning, he was in the thick of it.
Armed with a knife he stood on a ladder,
slicing through woody flesh
as beads of sweat trickled down his nose
and decorated his beard like diamonds,
glimmering sharply in the pale autumn light.

He paid no attention as the bramble fought back,
etching hard patterns criss-crossing his skin,
and bleeding blackberry juice everywhere –
staining his clothes, his hat,
smarting the vermilion scratches
that covered his face and arms.

He returned to the house around about dusk,
crashing through the back door,
clothes ripped to shreds, a wild look in his eye,
the knife gripped firmly in his teeth,
one bloodied arm held aloft.
And in his hand, a hatful of berries,
thick juice oozing through his fingers.

Hunter's Moon

She appeared from nowhere
to stand by his campfire,
wearing a green
raggedy dress and no shoes.
Her hair was the colour of earth.

And when she opened her mouth,
the words came out
as silver thread,
embroidering the night sky,
and joining dotted stars.

He tried to understand her,
but the words were foreign
to his untrained eye,
while his own words
were stones in his throat.

All the night-time creatures
read the words in the sky,
and came from miles around
to congregate in silence
by the light of the fire.

When a wolf appeared,
he wasn't afraid
as it sat right in front of him;
it's eyes like hot coals,
burning right into his.

And then he read
the silver letters in the sky
as if he had spoken them;
while a hunter's moon,
just behind the trees,

watched the night unfold.

Fire Lives with Me

There was fire,
mountains of fire upon fire.
It licked under the door
with flame red tongues,
and left charcoal kisses on the carpet.

It filled my windows
and melted the glass
so everything looked wrong.
It had burned through the air,
making breathing hard work.

Somehow, I felt
that the fire belonged to me;
that it was trying to come home;
blazing a trail across the sky
from somewhere far away.

And so I let it in.
I opened the door and invited
the sky high fire into my house.
And it settled on the hearthrug,
as a low and flickering flame.

We spoke at length
in reds, oranges and blues;
the parched air a chalk-board
for our words
that stretched to the ceiling and walls.

And now fire lives with me again
in my newly gutted house.
We decorated it together,
branding it
with blackened words.

Breathing

There is no air here.
I take tiny sips, desperately;
each mouthful is not enough.
A wind blows high in the trees,
so I stand on my toes,
and try to breathe it in.

But this is no use,
so I climb high into the trees.
I hang onto the highest
thin branches as the breeze
takes them, holds them,
ebbs and flows.

I have hollow bones.
I have a song that is
almost imperceptible,
I have lungfuls of air.
I am quite light-headed.
I have painted feathers.

And now I am hanging on
to the treetop for all I'm worth,
as the wind gets stronger.
It blows my feathers inside out,
and as I gulp for breath
it steals my voice.

One hiccup and I'm tumbling
through branches,
feathers flying all over the place;
my wingless arms flail in space.
And my voice says;
you do not belong there.

And it is my voice,
and it is breathless
as it follows me down to the ground,
just inside my ear.
That's better, it chokes
between gasps, *that's better.*

The Sky Wolf

That night the moon came up as usual.
Nocturnal creatures made
their customary music,
and people drew their curtains
and lit their lamps and fires.

The wolf that chases the sun
had made good ground for once;
with one snap of his awesome jaw,
he swallowed it whole,
singeing his fur a little in the process.

By day the moon was a distant ghost
in the still dark sky,
and people lit their lamps again
and tried to go about their business.
The day was long and as cold as night.

As night fell, the moon lit up the land
and they walked outside
just to bathe in its light.
Owls swooped overhead by day
and flowers pressed their petals shut.

The wolf was pursuing the moon by now,
snapping at its aura.
People watched and feared the worst;
crowding together on hills and mountains,
appealing to the gods for mercy.

All at once a spear of lightning
ripped the wolf from tail to snout.
His blood rained down in fire and ash,
filling the seas and drowning the land.
And then there was dark and silence.

Later, dawn broke across the world.
The last remaining tree
held its leaves to the sun. The birds
and creatures that were sheltering there
walked in the light once more.

And in the sky a wolf uncurled,
hungrily scanning the stars.

The Weight of a Hundred Babies

When, like a ravening wolf,
fire ate everything in sight, turning crops
into charcoal and air into poison,
all the pregnant women of the land
gave birth to fireflies.

And in their thousands
these tiny amber lights
danced above the burning towns
moving higher and higher
till there was no smoke to dull them.

The women wrung their hands in grief
as they watched their children
soar far out of sight;
they knew they were lost forever
to the star-spattered sky.

Years passed and the land became dead;
no crops would grow
in the blackened earth,
and no children were born.
People grew older and sadder.

Then one day, a miracle;
it began to rain.
Every drop was huge,
like a giant bubble reflecting colours
of the time before fire.

Wherever a drop landed,
a tree or a clump of grass,
or a flower sprung from the ground.
If it fell in the arms of a woman,
it became a new baby smelling of dew.

The women blessed the sun
and the stars and the moon,
as they juggled the babies in their arms,
crushed by the weight
of the hundreds they were trying to catch.